M000221900

The Long Sword Gloss of
GNM Manuscript 3227a

The Long Sword Gloss of GNM Manuscript 3227a

Michael Chidester

HEMA Bookshelf

Published by HEMA Bookshelf, LLC
411a Highland Ave #141
Somerville, MA, 02144
www.hemabookshelf.com

Version 2.0, 2021

ISBN 978-1-953683-13-7

Typeset in Libertinus Serif Display and Libertinus Sans, which are used
under the Open Font License
http://libertine-fonts.org/

Contents

Introduction

About the Ms. 3227a

The **Pol Hausbuch** (ms. 3227a) is a German commonplace book (or *Hausbuch*) thought to have been created some time between 1389 and 1494. The original currently rests in the holdings of the Germanisches Nationalmuseum in Nuremberg, Germany.[1]

It's sometimes erroneously attributed to Hans (or "Hanko") Döbringer, when in fact he is but one of the four authors of a brief addendum to Johannes Liechtenauer's art of unarmored long sword fencing, which is also the only fencing material in the manuscript that appears in another fencing manual.[2]

What's more, the scribe who created this manuscript actually forgot to include Döbringer's name in that section, and had to insert it after the fact, leading JEFFREY FORGENG to comment once that if there's one person in the world who we can assume *didn't* write this book, it was the person whose name was skipped.[3]

Still, due to the long identification with Hans Döbringer, the anonymous author of this text is sometimes called "Pseudo-Döbringer", and the manuscript itself Codex Döbringer. I prefer to name it the Pol Hausbuch after its first known owner, Doctor Nicolaus Pol.

Assigning a date to the manuscript is equally problematic. It's often said to have been written in 1389,[4] based on a table

---

[1] For more information about the ms. 3227a, see "Pol Hausbuch (MS 3227a)". *Wiktenauer.* http://wiktenauer.com/wiki/Pol_Hausbuch_(MS_3227a)

[2] Item # E.1939.65.341 at the Kelvingrove Museum in Glasgow. See "Glasgow Fechtbuch (MS E.1939.65.341)". *Wiktenauer.* http://wiktenauer.com/wiki/Glasgow_Fechtbuch_(MS_ E.1939.65.341)

[3] Public lecture.

[4] As in ŻABIŃSKI 2008 and LINDHOLM et al. "Cod. HS. 3227a, or Hanko Döbringer fechtbuch from 1389". 2005.

on folio 83^v which lists the number of Sundays between Epiphany and Ash Wednesday for the years 1390-1495 (often incorrectly described as a calendar). This misunderstands the nature of commonplace books like this, in which resources were copied onto their pages without necessarily being modified for relevance. Such tables were generally used by priests for planning sermons, and as long as it contained the years needed by its owner (or intended owner), there was no need to chop off years that had already passed or that were far in the future.

A more reliable date was offered by ONDŘEJ VODIČKA based on analysis of the script. Though he acknowledges that the date of 1389 is within the realm of possibility, he indicates that it's most likely that the manuscript was written in the first third of the 15th century.[5] This lines up nicely with the inclusion of contents like *Liber Ignis*, which was very rare in the late 14th century but much easier to come by in the early 15th.

The manuscript 3227a is a strange book, full of advice and recipes on all sorts of mundane and esoteric topics, ranging fencing and grappling to medicine and magic. In this way, it is typical of 15th century commonplace books, which tended to contain anything and everything that their owners found to be interesting.

The martial sections of the text consist of commentary (or gloss) on and expansion of the teachings of Liechtenauer, including other weapons not taught anywhere else such as sword and buckler, Messer, staff, dagger, and unarmed grappling. It also includes the only biographical details about the

---

[5] VODIČKA 2019.

grand master yet discovered, and it's even possible that he was still alive at the time of its writing.

What makes Pseudo-Döbringer's writings most important is their uniqueness. Where the glosses of Sigmund Ainringck, Pseudo-Peter von Danzig, Lew, and Nicolaus are all based on a single (lost) original gloss, and that of Hans Medel is borrows heavily from Ainringck and Nicolaus, Pseudo-Döbringer's teachings show no awareness of or influence from any other text in the tradition (except the teachings in the addendum mentioned above). Instead, he presents a fresh perspective on Liechtenauer's teachings, and even brings traces of the scholastic tradition to the study of fencing.[6]

Furthermore, his writings on weapons other than the sword are the only evidence that Liechtenauer might have had teachings beyond what is contained in the Recital. It's possible, of course, that this author had only a tenuous connection to the Liechtenauer tradition and that he attributed teachings to it which were completely alien. We will probably never know.

A Deeper Cut

A little of the strangeness of ms. 3227a can be explained by understanding how it was made. For this description, I will be essentially recapping and combining the analyses published by ERIC BURKART in 2016[7] and by ONDŘEJ VODIČKA in 2019,[8] and adding some of my own commentary. If this interests you, you should read their papers next.

---

[6] See J. ACUTT. *Swords, Science, and Society*. Fallen Rook Publishing, 2019.
[7] BURKART 2016.
[8] VODIČKA 2019.

The manuscript consists of 166 leaves of paper and 3 of parchment (169 total). It is a tiny manuscript, measuring just 100 mm × 140 mm (4 × 5 ½ inches). The binding is a modern reproduction of a Medieval binding, with leather over wooden boards. A piece of tooled leather from the original front cover was preserved and is now mounted on the new cover. It has a single clasp, which might also have been preserved from the original binding.

The author of the manuscript 3227a is unknown, as I said earlier. He was clearly a fencer with some understanding of the teachings of Johannes Liechtenauer, though whether you consider him a fencing master with a deep understanding of the subject or merely a student with wild ideas will typically come down to how much you like his interpretations. BURKART assumes that the manuscript was written by this fencing master personally, but VODIČKA argues convincingly that this is not the case, and rather the master was dictating his commentary to a scribe.

In either case, the manuscript was largely written by a single scribe (apart from a note on folio 157^v by Nicolaus Pol). The rubrics (red text) seem to be in the same handwriting, but the larger red letters were added by a different rubricator based on tiny guide letters included by the scribe. This artist seems to have not understood or not cared about the text (since in a few places he drew the wrong letter, mangling the words).

There are two sets of page numbers, and they offer the first clues about the original composition of the manuscript. The back of each leaf (or *verso* side) is numbered in red ink in a 15th century script, whereas the front of each leaf (or *recto* side) is numbered in pencil by a modern hand. Figure 8 includes both page numbers for comparison.

These page numbers don't match up, and the gaps in the red numbering show us where pages were present early on and have since disappeared; the red numbers are written to fit around the text, showing that they were added after the manuscript was complete. In total, 21 numbered pages are missing from the current manuscript (see figure 8), though as we'll see in a minute, others probably went missing before the red numbers were added.

The manuscript currently consists of twelve quires (stacks of paper that are folded in half to create two pages per sheet); the first ten each contain 13-17 folia (half-sheets) and appear to be part of the original plan of the manuscript, whereas the eleventh is a bundle of twenty-one single leaves that were glued together, and the twelfth is much shorter (only 8 folia) and was added to hold the index.

Only the first seven quires hold fencing teachings, so those are the ones I will focus on here. To make all this number juggling easier, I will refer to these quires by the Roman numerals that you see in the figures.

These details about the composition of the manuscript may seem dry, but they hold clues that can tell us a story about the process by which it was constructed.

Before the book was bound, each quire seems to have been assembled and treated as a small booklet, and some or all of the booklets had parchment covers. Most of the text was written in these booklets before they were bound together into a single book, and this allowed the scribe to fit more text on each page (Medieval bindings are very tight, and part of each page by the spine is generally inaccessible after binding). It's unclear whether the booklets were all created and intended for this manuscript from the beginning, or whether the scribe simply had a supply of them and added more as the contents of the manuscript grew.

The various pieces of writing in the manuscript never cross from one booklet to another, so individual quires are useful units to talk about in analyzing the text.

Manuscript 3227a was created in at least four phases.

In the first phase, the author dictated the text of Liechtenauer's Recital and the scribe recorded it in three booklets (quires II–IV), planning out space for the commentary on each section. Assuming the author had committed the Recital to memory (as most Liechtenauer fencers would have), it would certainly have made the most sense to begin with the part that he could rattle off effortlessly.

The mounted and armored verses receive much less blank space than the unarmored verses, so if commentary was planned for them, the scribe expected it to be brief. The unarmored verses are broken into the same standard sections as other glosses and statements of the Recital, but the amount of space left for each one varies considerably. Sometimes two sections were written on the same page, allowing only a quarter of a page for commentary on each, and other times up to five and a half pages were left blank.

In the first pass, the scribe already included some extra verses that are not part of Liechtenauer's original Recital, apparently unique inventions of the author.

Once the verse was laid out, the second phase began. The author went back and began to add commentary for each segment. He jumped around a lot, skipping back and forth, and ultimately only added commentary for about half of the sections. This phase may also have been when two more booklets (VI and VII) were added and the plan was made for treatises on the buckler, staff, Messer, dagger, and wrestling; each section received an introductory paragraph, with blank space left for more commentary. (This could instead have been part of the first phase.)

The second phase is also when the treatise of the "other masters" (Andres Juden, Jobs von der Nyssen, Nicklass Prewßen, and "the Priest" Hans Döbringer) was written into the manuscript (10-15 of quire III and 5 of quire IV). This was probably a written record that the author had access to and wanted to include in his book, but it was potentially abridged during the copying. The text covers less than half of the blank pages allotted to it, and it includes a statement early on that many of the techniques of the masters had been omitted and only a few which were relevant for school fencing (from the iron gate) would be included.

In the third phase, the author went back and began to correct and expand the commentary from the second phase. It's unclear why this started before the initial commentary was completed.

Where the text from the second phase is fairly tidy and the pages are laid out neatly with small but comfortable margins, the third phase destroys that plan. Notes were written into the margins with carrots or lines indicating where they fit into the text. Extra verses were added into parts of the Recital. The writing in general is smaller and more cramped. When the author wanted to include a different poem about the virtues of fencing (possibly of his own devising), the scribe wrote it onto the blank cover of quire II.

In the general teaching, the author was apparently not satisfied with his explanation of the Five Words and the Leading Strike but had no more room to expand it, so the scribe pulled an entire bifolium (two-page sheet) from elsewhere and inserted it into quire II as two extra pages. This is where the author introduces the Following Strike as a counterpart to the Leading Strike, and the only place where he quotes Aristotle.

The third phase is also when quire I was added to hold the introduction, and quire V to hold the conclusion. The author began his commentary on the other weapons in this phase, describing wrestling, dagger, and Messer in varying levels of detail, but doesn't seem to have reached the buckler and staff teachings.

After the third phase, the commentary was clearly not complete, but the scribe seems to no longer have had access to the author. Perhaps he died, perhaps he moved to a different city, or perhaps he was just broke and no longer able to pay for the book.

Whatever the reason, the fourth phase consists of the scribe filling out the rest of the manuscript—the beginning of quire I and the remainder of quires V-X—with suitably esoteric contents (alchemy, medicine, magic, etc.) that would make it sellable. The fact that the scribe didn't fill in any of the blank pages inside the fencing section suggests that perhaps the author was still alive, and the scribe hoped that at some point he would return to finish those sections.

Once the fourth phase was complete, the manuscript was bound. The ten quires of the original plan were joined by a stack of miscellaneous pages as quire XI and a short final index in quire XII. Only quires II and XII (and perhaps I) kept their parchment covers, and the back cover to II was later torn out. Around this time, the red page numbers were added, though a few pages had already fallen or been torn out by that time.

The rough state of the pages, with rounded corners and worn edges, tells us that the manuscript was probably used and carried quite a bit in its early years, and also that it might have first been bound in an inexpensive limp leather binding and only later received protective wooden boards.

About This Book

What you hold in your hands is a rendering of the anonymous gloss of Liechtenauer's verses on long sword fencing (fencing with both hands on the grip) from 3227a. I have omitted the writings of Döbringer and the other masters, as well as the other teachings attributed to Liechtenauer, in order to focus on one specific thread in this tapestry.

My primary intent with this translation was to produce a readable text that untangles a lot of the convoluted phrasing and conveys the core ideas as clearly as possible. This is a departure from my usual translation style—I actually love convoluted phrasing—but this text is so dense that it's hard to make sense of it any other way.

I prepared it for use in my gloss compilation project, where I reimagine Pseudo-Döbringer as an owner and marginal commentator on a copy of the combined Ainringck-Danzig-Lew-Nicolaus gloss. Some who saw it there asked for it to be released separately (and in an easier-to-read format), so here we are. I won't claim that this translation is as easy to read as other similar entries in the market, such as HARRY R.'s recent publication of the anonymous gloss of Pseudo-Peter von Danzig,[9] but I've done my best to put together a text that says what the author was trying to say in the clearest way I could.

This manuscript is extraordinarily dense and difficult, and in preparing this translation (and untangling the language) I relied heavily on the marvelous transcriptions of DIERK

---

[9] R., HARRY. *Peter von Danzig*. Blurb.com, 2019.
http://www.blurb.com/b/9442168-peter-von-danzig

HAGEDORN,[10] a revised and corrected version of which is included in this volume, and ONDŘEJ VODIČKA.[11]

I'm also deeply indebted to the pioneering work in the first years of the 21st century by DAVID LINDHOLM (and friends),[12] THOMAS STOEPPLER,[13] and GRZEGORZ ŻABIŃSKI,[14] as well as more recent efforts at translation and analysis by JENS P. KLEINAU[15] and CHRISTIAN TROSCLAIR (whose translation currently graces the Wiktenauer article).[16]

Rather than produce my own translation of Liechtenauer's core Recital, I have instead relied on a version of HARRY's remarkable rhyming translation (modified in places to better match my gloss translation and to remove the German words he sometimes uses). I chose this over a more literal translation, even though some meaning might be lost, for two reasons: first, because the Recital is not intended to convey meaning without the gloss (or without instruction from someone who understands it), so that's not much of a loss,

---

[10] HAGEDORN, DIERK. "HS. 3227A". *Hammaborg Historischer Schwertkampf,* 2008. http://www.hammaborg.de/en/transkriptionen/3227a/index.php

[11] VODIČKA, ONDŘEJ. "Transcription of GNM Hs. 3227a". Wiktenauer. https://wiktenauer.com/wiki/File:Vodicka_Hs-3227a-transcription_ver17.pdf

[12] LINDHOLM, DAVID et al. "Cod.HS.3227a, or Hanko Döbringer fechtbuch from 1389". 2005. http://www.hroarr.com/manuals/liechtenauer/Dobringer_A5_sidebyside.pdf

[13] STOEPPLER, THOMAS. Private communication, 2006. Used in "Pol Hausbuch (MS 3227a)". *Wiktenauer.* 2013-2018.

[14] ŻABIŃSKI, GRZEGORZ. "Unarmored Longsword Combat by Master Liechtenauer via Priest Döbringer". *Masters of Medieval and Renaissance Martial Arts.* Ed. JEFFREY HULL. Boulder, CO: Paladin Press, 2008.

[15] KLEINAU, JENS P. Several articles. *Hans Talhoffer ~ A Historical Martial Arts blog by Jens P. Kleinau.* 2011-2015. http://talhoffer.wordpress.com/category/readable-manuscripts/gmn-3227a/

[16] TROSCLAIR, CHRISTIAN. Private communication, 2018. Used in "Pol Hausbuch (MS 3227a)". *Wiktenauer.* 2018-present.

and second, because having a rhyming poem explained in prose might give a tiny glimpse of the intended experience of a 15th century German learning Liechtenauer's art. Unfortunately, my own skills as a poet are not sufficient to attempt a similar rhyming translation of the unique verses in 3227a.

No translation can ever be truly unbiased. That said, 3227a, even more than most texts, stubbornly refuses a generic or neutral reading. All of the translations mentioned above are reflections of the interpretations of their authors, and mine is no different. Please forgive my mistakes as they become apparent in the future. HEMA is a journey of discovery for all of us.

It is my hope that this translation can now speak for itself, so I will offer only one small piece of interpretive advice. I once believed that Pseudo-Döbringer was presenting a unique interpretation of Liechtenauer's teachings, but after this work, it seems clear to me that his writings are very much in line with the teachings of other early glossators, and only his terminology differs much.

The core device of Pseudo-Döbringer's writings, the *Vorschlag* (leading strike) and *Nachschlag* (following strike), is not a unique teaching at all, but merely a more verbose treatment of Liechtenauer's general teaching. If you take and follow all of the advice in the general teaching at once (striking from your strong without waiting for your opponent's action, strike Before your opponent, remain with your point in front of his face so you threaten him and he must parry, and then follow up on your attack with a hit to the nearest exposure), then you will be performing the leading strike and following strike in accordance with this teaching.

Indeed, it seems to me that even though the other glosses break the general teaching up into 5-6 chunks, they also intend you to apply it all at once, and simply lack a handy name to describe it.

In general, I recommend that you come to this text with two assumptions. First, that it is in general agreement with the other five glosses and the points of disagreement are minor. Second, that you don't understand the other five glosses nearly as well as you think you do, and Pseudo-Döbringer has lessons to teach you about them.

About the Translation

While my translation style usually tends toward the cryptographic (or a fairly direct 1:1 relationship between the original text and the translation), I have tried a different approach here. I made no effort to preserve German word order or speech patterns, clauses are moved around or collapsed together, and sometimes whole sentences are out of order. (Furthermore, words are often translated differently in different places.)

Where marginal notes are inserted into the main text, this is indicated by the given symbol (usually a † or #) followed by {curly brackets} containing the inserted text. Latin words and phrases are rendered in *italics*.

Pseudo-Döbringer is notable among Liechtenauer authors because he expands the Recital to almost twice its typical length. In this book, lines of the standard Recital are given in black ink and assigned their couplet number (from 1 to 109), while extra lines appear in grey ink and are given Roman numerals. (Some verses appear several times, and they are given the same numeral in each.)

Finally, it is a custom in our community to leave certain magic words untranslated. I despise this practice and believe that the translator's job is to translate, so I have not left any

German words in my translation. Instead, you will find such words rendered in **bold** text. This also allows me to present multiple translations for the same word in different places, and to use them as different parts of speech.

Introduction

The Text

Some glosses, especially those in the pseudo-Peter von Dan-
zig branch, clearly demarcate the "Text", by which they mean
Liechtenauer's Recital, and the "Gloss", by which they mean
the commentary and interpretation of the Recital.

Manuscript 3227a does not list the text of the Recital on
long sword fencing in its own section separate from the gloss,
but I've decided to list it separately anyway for easier com-
parison and reference.

* * * * *

**This is the general preface of the unarmored fencing on
foot. Remember it well.**

1   Young knight learn onward,
     For god have love, and ladies, honor,

2   Till your honor is earned,
     Practice chivalry, and learn,

3   Let the art grace you wholly,
     And in war bring you glory.

4   Wrestle well, grappler;
     Lance, spear, sword, and dagger,

5   Wield them, be brazen,
     In others' hands raze them.

6   Cut in and close fast,
     Advance to meet, or let it past.

7   Earn the envy of the wise,
     Win boundless praise before your eyes.

8   Therefore here behold the way,
     Every art is measured, weighed.

i   And whatever you wish to do,
     Shall stay in the realm of good reason.

ii   In earnest or in play,
       Have a joyous spirit, but in moderation

iii   So that you may pay attention
       And perform with a good spirit

iv   Whatever you shall do
       And whip up against him.

v   Because a good spirit with force
       Makes your resistance dauntless.

vi   Thereafter, conduct yourself so that
       You give no advantage with anything.

vii   Avoid imprudence.
       Don't engage four or six

viii   With your overconfidence.
       Be modest, that is good for you.

ix   It's a bold man
       Who dares to confront his equal,

x   But it's not shameful
       To flee from four or six at hand.

This is the general teaching of the sword.

9   To have the art within your sight,
       Set left forth and cut with right,

10   You will find that left with right
       Is the strongest way for you to fight.

11   He who waits for cuts and follows,
       In this art finds naught but sorrow.

12   A nearing cut is good to do,
       Your shield to stop him changing through.

xi   † {Do not cut toward his sword,
       But rather seek out his exposures.}

13	Toward head and body and the head,
	And the flesh-wounds do not forget.
14	With your whole body shall you fight,
	For that is how you fence with might.
15	Another rule you should not slight:
	Fence not from left when you are right.
16	If with your left is how you fight,
	You'll fence much weaker from the right.
xii	So always prefer to fence
	Downward from the left side.
17	Before and After, these two things,
	Which are to all arts a wellspring.
18	Likewise there is Weak and Strong,
	And the word 'Within', remember hereon.
19	You can learn, then,
	With skill, to work and defend.
20	If you easily take fright,
	You shouldn't ever learn to fight.
xiii	Audacity and speed,
	prudence, cunning and ingenuity,
xiv	†† {Reason, stealth,
	moderation, deliberation, readiness;}
xv	Fencing must have all of this
	and carry a joyous spirit.

This is the text in which he names the five strikes and the other pieces of his fencing.

21	Learn five strikes,
	To the guard from the right.

23[17]   Wrath strike curves thwarts,
         Has glancing with parts.
24   While the fool will parry,
         Pursue, overrun, stab and harry.
25   Pull back and disengage,
         Run through, press hands, and slice away.
26   Hang and wind to exposures below and above,
         Strike and catch, sweep, and thrust with a shove.

This is about the wrathful cut, etc.

27   Who cuts from above in any way,
         The wrathful cut's point keeps him at bay.
28   If he sees and fends you off,
         Be fearless, take it off above.
29   Wind and thrust if he holds strong so;
         If he sets you off, take it below.
30   Now remember this part:
         Cut and thrust, lay Soft or Hard;
31   Within the Before and the After,
         Be careful, and do not rush to the war.
32   Those who rashly seek the bind,
         Shame above and below is all they'll find.
33   Howsoever you will wind,
         Cut, thrust, slice you seek to find.
34   Further, you should learn to choose
         Which of them should best suit you.
35   In whatever way you've bound,
         Many masters you'll confound.

---

[17] Verse 22 is omitted for unknown reasons. It states, "And this we can promise / Your art will be glorious."

xi	Do not cut toward his sword,
	But rather seek his exposures.
xvi	Toward his head, toward his body,
	If you wish to remain unharmed.
xvii	Whether you hit or you miss,
	Always target his exposures.
xviii	* {In every lesson,
	Turn your point against his exposures.
xix	Whoever swings around widely,
	He will often be shamed severely.
xx	Toward the nearest exposure,
	Cut and thrust with suddenness.
xxi	And also step always
	Toward your right side with it,
xxii	So you may begin
	Fencing or wrestling with advantage.}

This is about the four exposures, etc., etc.

36	Four exposures know,
	To truly guide your blow.
37	Without fear or doubt,
	For what he'll bring about.

How to break the four exposures.

38	Redeem yourself by taking
	Four exposures by their breakings.
39	To above, you redouble,
	Transmute low without trouble.
40	Now do not forget,
	No one defends without a threat.

41   If this is well known,
            Rarely will he come to blows.

This is about the crooked cut, etc.

42   Throw the curve, and don't be slow,
            Onto his hands your point should go.

43   Many strikes you will offset,
            With a curve and with good steps.

44   Cut the curve to the flat,
            Weaken masters with that.

45   When it clashes above,
            Step off, that I will love.

46   Cut short, and curve not,
            If the changing through is sought.

47   Curve who'd distress you,
            Confuse, bind, and press him,

48   Give him no way to know
            Where he's safe from your blow.

[The Avoidance]

53   Avoid and mislead,
            Then hit low where you please.

54   The inverter equips you,
            To run through and grip, too.

55   Take the elbow to bring
            Him off balance, and spring.

56   Avoid twice;
            If you touch, make a slice.

57   Double it and on it goes,
            Step in left and don't be slow.

xxiii Because all fencing
       Will by rights have speed,
xiii   And also audacity,
       Prudence, cunning, and ingenuity.

This is about the crosswise cut, etc.

49 What comes from the sky,
    The cross takes in its stride.
50 Cut across with the strong,
    And be sure to work on.
51 To the plow drive across,
    Yoke it hard to the ox.
52 Take a leap and cross well,
    And his head is imperiled.

This is about the glancing cut.

58 The glancer disrupts
    What the buffalo cuts or thrusts.
59 The glancer endangers
    Whoever threatens the changer.
60 If he looks short to you,
    Defeat him by changing through.
61 To the point glance goes,
    Take his neck boldly so.
62 Glance up high instead
    To endanger his hands and head.
xxiv # {Glance to the right,
      If you want to fence well.
xxv   The glancing cut I prize,
      If it doesn't come too lazily.}

This is about the part cut, etc.

63   Strike from your part
            And threaten his face with art.

64   When it turns it will set
            On his chest with great threat.

65   What the parter brings forth,
            The crown drives it off,

66   So slice through the crown,
            And you break it well down.

67   Press the sweeping attacks,
            With a slice and pull back.

xxv   The part cut I prize,
            If it doesn't come too lazily.

This is about the four lairs, etc.

68   Lie in four lairs,
            And the others forswear.

69   Ox and plow, and the fool too,
            And the day should not be unknown to you.

xxvi   The fool always counters
            What the man cuts or thrusts

xxvii   With hanging, sweeps,
            Pursuit, and simultaneous parries.

This is about the four parries, etc., etc.

70   The parries are four,
            They leave lairs well sored.

71   Of parrying, beware:
            You should not be caught there.

72	If parrying befalls you,
	As it can happen to do,
73	Hear now what I say:
	Wrench off, slice away!
74	Set upon to four extents;
	Stay thereon if you want to end.
xxviii	# {*Many strikes you'll hurt and harry*
	If you fence with proper parries,[18]
xxix	Because when you parry,
	You come swiftly into the hangers.}

This is about pursuit, etc., etc.

75	Learn the twofold pursuit,
	And the guard, to slice through.
76	The ways to lead out are double,
	From there work and struggle.
77	And determine what he seeks,
	Hard or Soft in his techniques.
78	Learn to feel with discipline;
	The word that cuts deepest is 'Within'.
79	Learn the pursuit twice,
	If it touches, make a good old slice.
xxx	*In whatever way you've bound,*
	All the strong you will confound.[19]
xviii	In every lesson,
	Turn your point against his face.
xxxi	Pursue with your entire body
	So that your point stays on.

---

[18] This verse is phrased similarly to 43.
[19] This verse is phrased similarly to both 35 and 90.

xxxii   Also learn to swiftly wrench,
         So you may end well.

This is about crossing over. Fencer, notice it.

80   Whoever aims to take it below,
       By the crossing over, their folly show.

81   When it clashes above,
       Remain Strong, that I will love.

82   See your work be done,
       Or press doubly hard upon.

xxxiii   Whoever presses you down,
        Cross over him and strike sharply again.

xxxiv   From both sides cross over,
        And remember the slices.

This is about setting off. Learn this well.

83   The setting off, learn to do,
       That cuts and thrusts be ruined before you.

84   Whoever makes a thrust at you,
       Your point meets his and breaks it through.

85   From the right and from the left,
       Always meet him if you'll step.

xviii   In every lesson,
        Turn your point against his face.

This is about changing through, etc., etc.

86   Learn to change through,
       And cruelly thrust on both sides too.

87   All of those who seek the bind,
       Changing through will surely find.

xxxv   † {When you have changed through,
      strike, thrust, or wind, be not lax.

xxxvi   Do not cut toward his sword,
      change through and seek with that.}

This is about pulling back. Fencer, remember.

88   Step up close into the bind,
      Pull back, and what you seek you'll find.

89   Pull back, and if he meets, pull more,
      Work and find what makes him sore.

90   Pull back whenever you are bound,
      And many masters you'll confound.

xxxvii   Pull back from the sword
      And carefully consider your way.

This is about running through, notice now.

91   Run through, hang it to the floor
      By the pommel, then bring grips for sure.

92   For those who strongly approach you,
      Do remember the running through.

xxxviii   Run through and shove.
      Invert if he grabs for the hilt.

This is about slicing off, etc., etc.

93   When it's firm, slice away,
      From below, you slice both ways.

94   And the slices, they number four,
      Two below; above, two more.

xxxix   Slice whoever will cross you,
      To eagerly avoid injury.

xl	Do not slice in fright,
	First consider wrenching.
xli	You can slice well in any crossing,
	If you omit the wrenching.
xlii	If you wish to remain unharmed,
	Then don't move with the slicing.

This is about pressing the hands, etc., etc.

95	Turn your edge just like that,
	Press his hands onto the flat.
xliii	One thing is turning,
	Another is twisting, the third is hanging.
xliv	If you want to make fencers despair,
	Then always press while shoving.
xlv	Over his hands,
	Cut and slice swiftly.
xlvi	Also draw the slices
	Above, over his head.
xlvii	Whoever presses the hands
	Pulls his fingers back without injury.

This is about hanging. Fencer, learn this, etc.

96	There are the two ways to hang:
	From the ground, from your hand.
97	In every attack, whether cut or a thrust,
	The Hard and the Soft lie within, you can trust.
98	In the window freely stand,
	Watch his manner close at hand.
99	Whoever pulls back,
	Strike in with a snap.

100	Now do not forget
	No one defends without a threat.
101	And if this is well-known,
	Rarely will he come to blows.
xlviii	As you remain,
	On the sword, then also make
xlix	Cuts, thrusts, or slices.
	Remember to feel into it
l	Without any preference.
	Also do not flee from the sword
li	Because masterful fencing
	Is rightly at the sword.
lii	Whoever binds on you,
	The war wrestles with him severely.
liii	The noble winding
	Can also surely find him.
liv	With cutting, with thrusting,
	And with slicing you surely find him.
[32]	*Howsoever you will wind,*
	Cut, thrust, slice you seek to find.
lv	And the noble hanging
	Should not be without the winding.
lvi	Because from the hangers
	You bring forth the winding.

[Winding] [20]

108	On both sides this applies:
	Learn to step with eight winds.
106	And each wind of the blade
	Into three can be made:
107	Twenty-four can be named,
	Though they're one and the same.
105	And eight winds there are,
	If you rightly regard,
lviii	And learn to lead them well,
	So you may hit the four exposures.
lix	Because each exposure
	Can be hit in six ways.

---

[20] This is the only place in the treatise where verses from the Recital are presented out of order. Furthermore, verses 102-104 are omitted entirely, as is 109 (though 109 is itself a repetition of verse 77). Here is the original sequence:

If you lead well, and counter right,
And finally, it's in your sight,
You must divide things as they are,
Into three wounders, each apart.
Hang the point in true and fair,
Wind your sword then well from there.
And eight winds there are,
If you rightly regard,
And each wind of blade
Into three can be made:
Twenty-four can be named,
Though they're one and the same.
On both sides this applies:
Learn to step with eight winds.
And determine what he seeks,
Hard or Soft in his techniques.

The gloss

What follows is the text and gloss of the Recital by pseudo-Hans Döbringer, beginning with a much longer introduction than any other gloss.

* * * * *

Here begins Master Liechtenauer's art of fencing with the sword, on horse and on foot, armored and unarmored. First and foremost, you should notice and remember that there's only one art of the sword, and it was discovered and developed hundreds of years ago, and it is the foundation and core of all fighting arts.

Master Liechtenauer understood and practiced this art completely and correctly; he did not discover or invent it himself (as has been written previously),[21] but rather traveled through many lands and searched for the true and correct art for the sake of experiencing and knowing it.

For this art is serious, correct, and complete, and everything that proceeds from it goes toward whatever is nearest by the shortest way, simply and directly.

When you want to cut or thrust at someone, it should be as if you tied a thread or a cord to the point or edge of your sword and pulled or drew it toward his nearest exposure, because you should cut or thrust in the shortest and surest

---

[21] Here the author seems to be referring to (and disagreeing with) an earlier writing about Liechtenauer which stated that he invented the art of fencing. There's no way to know what writing this is referring to, but the glosses of Sigmund Ainringck, Pseudo-Peter von Danzig, and Nicolaus all make this claim, and it is therefore likely to have come from the original ur-gloss of that tradition. If that is what the author is referring to, it is yet another sign that this gloss was written in the 15th century (and also evidence that the author had access to those teachings, even though he didn't incorporate them into his gloss).

manner, in the most decisive way. This is all you should want to do, because proper fencing doesn't have broad or elaborate parries, nor the wide fencing around by which people procrastinate and delay.

You will still find many dancing masters[22] claiming that they believe that the art of the sword grows better and richer from day to day, and that they have conceived and created a new art. But I would like to see anyone who could invent and perform a legitimate strike or play that falls outside of Liechtenauer's art. All they do is jumble and confuse the plays and then give them new names (each according to his own ideas), and they devise wide parries and often want to do two or three strikes in place of a single one.

They do this to be praised by the ignorant for the sheer liveliness of it, as they stand fiendishly and perform elaborate parries and wide fencing around, and, having no moderation in their fencing, they bring long and far-reaching strikes, slowly and clumsily, and severely delay and overextend and expose themselves. This doesn't belong to earnest fencing, but only to play in the fencing schools for exercise and entertainment.

Earnest fencing goes swiftly and precisely, without hesitation or delay, as if measured and balanced by a cord (or something similar). When you cut or thrust at the man who stands in front of you, then clearly no strike backwards or to the side can help you, nor any wide fencing with multiple strikes (nor

---

[22] *Leichmeister* is a pun that I can't capture in English: *leich* means a dance or other rhythmic movement, and *leiche* means corpse.

Leichmeister seem to be masters who teach fencing that is more like dancing than fighting, and get their students killed if they ever have to fight a duel. "Masters of the deadly dance" might capture the double meaning, but it makes them sound awesome which is hardly the intent.

any other way that you procrastinate and delay, and miss the chance to end it with him).

On the contrary, you must strike straight and directly toward him (toward his head or body, whatever is nearest and surest), so that you can reach and take him swiftly and rapidly. Furthermore, one strike is better than delivering four or six, delaying and waiting too long so your opponent wins the Leading Strike faster than you (because this strike is a great advantage in fencing).

It's written further on in the text how Liechtenauer only lists five strikes, along with other plays which are sufficient for earnest fencing, and he teaches how to perform them according to the true art, straight and direct, as closely and as certainly as possible. Moreover, he leaves aside all the new inventions and confusing work of the dancing masters, which don't come from this art.

Now notice and remember that you can't speak or write about fencing and explain it as simply and clearly as it can be shown and taught by hand. Therefore, you should consider and debate matters in your mind—and practice them even more in play—so that you understand them in earnest fencing. Practice is better than artfulness, because practice could be sufficient without artfulness, but artfulness is never sufficient without practice.

Also know that the sword is like a set of scales, so that if the blade is large and heavy, the pommel must also be heavy (just as with scales). Therefore, to use your sword certainly and securely, grip it with both hands between the guard and the pommel, because you hold the sword with much more certainty like this than when you grip it with one hand on the pommel. You also strike much harder and more strongly, because the pommel overthrows itself and swings itself in harmony with the strike, and the strike then arrives much harder than when you grip the sword by the pommel (which restrains the pommel so that the strike can't come strongly or correctly).

Furthermore, when you fence with someone, take full heed of your steps and be certain in them, just as if you were standing on a set of scales, moving backward or forward as necessary, firmly and skillfully, swiftly and readily.

Your fencing should proceed with good spirit and good mind or reason, and without fear (as is written later).

You should also have moderation in your plays and not step too far, so that you can better recover from one step to the next (backward or forward, however they go). Also, two short steps are often faster than one long one, so you will need to do a little run with short steps as often as you will a big step or a leap.

Whatever you want to perform cleverly, in earnest or in play, should be hidden from the eyes of your opponent so that he doesn't know what you intend to do to him.

As soon as you approach the point where you believe you could very well reach and take him, step and strike toward him brazenly, and then drive swiftly toward his head or body. You must always win the Leading Strike, whether it lands or misses, and thus allow him to come to nothing (as is written better further on in the general teaching).

Moreover, it's better to target the upper exposures rather than the lower, and then boldly and swiftly drive in over his hilt with cuts or thrusts, since you can reach him much better and more certainly over his hilt than under it. You're also much surer in all your fencing like this, for an upper hit is much better than a lower one. Though if it happens that the lower exposures are nearer (as it often does), then you should target them.

Always go to your right side with your plays, because in all matters of fencing and wrestling, you can better take your opponent in this way than directly from the front. Whoever knows this piece and brings it well is not a bad fencer.

Remember that if you're required to fight earnestly, you should contemplate a thoroughly-practiced play beforehand (whichever you want, if it's complete and correct), and internalize it seriously and hold it in your mind with good spirit. Then perform whatever you chose upon your opponent with pure intent (just as if you were to say, "This I truly intend to do well"), and it should and must go forward with the aid of God, so it will fail you in nothing. Thus you do righteously by charging and stepping in to strike the Leading Strike (as it's written many times further on).

The Gloss

[23]Oh, all fighting requires
The help of the God of Righteousness,
A straight and healthy body,
And a complete and well-made sword.
Before, After, Strong, Weak;
'Within', remember that word;
Cuts, thrusts, slices, pressing,
Guards, covers, pushing, feeling, pulling back,
Winding and hanging,
Moving in and out, leaping, grabbing, wrestling,
Speed and audacity,
Prudence, cunning and ingenuity,
Moderation, stealth,
Reason, deliberation, readiness,
Exercise and good spirit,
Motion, dexterity, good steps.
In these several verses
Are fundamentals, principles
And concerns,
And the entire matter
Of all the art of fencing is labelled for you.
You should consider this correctly,
As you will also actually,
And in particular hereafter,
Hear or read it,
In an exact and precise manner.
Fencer, understand this,
So will be revealed to you the complete art
Of the whole sword,
And many good and lively attacks.

---

[23] This poem and paragraph were added after the rest of the text.

'Motion', that beautiful word,
Is the heart of fencing, and the crown.
The whole matter
Of fencing, with all
The concerns and articles
Of the foundation, which
Are called by their names,
Will be revealed to you hereafter.
When you fight,
Be well familiar with them,
And stay in motion
And not at rest,
So that when fighting starts,
You do it correctly,
Continuously and decisively,
One after another, boldly,
In a continuous advance,
Immediately and with no pause,
So that your opponent cannot come
To blows. This way, you will profit
And the other will be harmed.
Because he can't escape
Without being beaten,
As long as you fence according to this advice
And according to the lesson,
Which is written in this way:
I say to you honestly,
No man covers himself without danger.
If you have understood this,
He cannot come to blows.[24]

---

[24] This quatrain is taken from the Recital, verses 40-41 and 100-101.

The Gloss

Here remember that *continual motion* is the beginning, the middle, and the end of all fencing according to this art and teaching, so that you strike the beginning, the middle, and the end in a single advance, and bring it well without the hindrance of your adversary and without allowing him to come to blows. This is based on the two words 'Before' and 'After' (that is, the Leading Strike and the Following Strike); *directly, in a single moment, one after another with nothing in between.*

This is the general preface of the unarmored fencing on foot. Remember it well.

1   Young knight learn onward,
         For god have love, and ladies, honor,

2   Till your honor is earned,
         Practice chivalry, and learn,

3   Let the art grace you wholly,
         And in war bring you glory.

4   Wrestle well, grappler;
         Lance, spear, sword, and dagger,

5   Wield them, be brazen,
         In others' hands raze them.

6   Cut in and close fast,
         Advance to meet, or let it past.

7   Earn the envy of the wise,
         Win boundless praise before your eyes.

8   Therefore here behold the way,
         Every art is measured, weighed.

i   And whatever you wish to do,
         Shall stay in the realm of good reason.

ii   In earnest or in play,
         Have a joyous spirit, but in moderation

iii   So that you may pay attention
         And perform with a good spirit

iv   Whatever you shall do
         And whip up against him.

v   Because a good spirit with force
         Makes your resistance dauntless.

vi   Thereafter, conduct yourself so that
         You give no advantage with anything.

The Gloss

vii	Avoid imprudence.
	Don't engage four or six
viii	With your overconfidence.
	Be modest, that is good for you.
ix	It's a bold man
	Who dares to confront his equal,
x	But it's not shameful
	To flee from four or six at hand.

This is the general teaching of the sword.

9   To have the art within your sight,
         Set left forth and cut with right,

10   You will find that left with right
         Is the strongest way for you to fight.

11   He who waits for cuts and follows,
         In this art finds naught but sorrow.

12   A nearing cut is good to do,
         Your shield to stop him changing through.

xi   † {Do not cut toward his sword,
         But rather seek out his exposures.}

13   Toward the body and the head,
         And the flesh-wounds do not forget.

14   With your whole body shall you fight,
         For that is how you fence with might.

15   Another rule you should not slight:
         Fence not from left when you are right.

16   If with your left is how you fight,
         You'll fence much weaker from the right.

xii   So always prefer to fence
         Downward from the left side.

17   Before and After, these two things,
         Which are to all arts a wellspring.

18   Likewise there is Weak and Strong,
         And the word 'Within', remember hereon.

19   You can learn, then,
         With skill, to work and defend.

20   If you easily take fright,
         You shouldn't ever learn to fight.

xiii   Audacity and speed,
         prudence, cunning and ingenuity,

A general gloss follows here.

First and foremost, notice and remember that the point of the sword is the center, the middle, and the core, which all fencing goes out from and comes back to. The hangers and the winds, which a lot of good fencing plays originate from, are the attaching and the revolving of the center and the core.

They were conceived and created so that if you cut or thrust exactly to the point, though you don't hit immediately, you might still hit your opponent with these plays: with cutting, thrusting, and slicing, and with stepping in and out, stepping around, and leaping.

If you mislay or overextend the point of your sword when shooting or lunging, you can recover and realign it by winding and stepping out, and thus come back to the reliable plays and rules of fencing, from which you can cut, thrust, or slice again. For all cutting, thrusting, and slicing can come from the plays and rules of the art of the sword, according to Liechtenauer's art.

(It's written further on how one play or rule results from another, and how to make one play out of another, so that as one of your strikes is defended, the next advances and succeeds.)

Moreover, notice and remember that no part of the sword was conceived or created without reason, so you should apply the point, both edges, the hilt and pommel, and everything which is on the sword, according to the specific role of each one in the art of fencing, and according to how you discover and embody the practice (as we will read in a more detailed manner hereafter).

Also notice and remember that when Liechtenauer says, "If you wish to see art", etc.,[25] he means to advance your left foot, and with that, cut threatening strikes from your right side (straight toward the man), just as soon as you see where you can take him and would certainly reach him by stepping.

He also means that when you want to fence strongly, fence with your left side leading, and with your entire body and strength, toward his head and body (whatever you can get) rather than toward his sword. In fact, you should strike as though he had no sword, or as though you couldn't see it, and you shouldn't disdain the flesh-wounds, but be always working and in motion so that he cannot come to blows.

He further means to not directly track and follow your cut with your feet, but rather move aside a little and curve around so that you come to your opponent's flank, since you can reach him more easily from there than from the front. When your cutting and thrusting goes directly toward his exposures (toward his head or body) while stepping or treading around him, then those strikes cannot be defended or diverted by changing through or other such plays.

Also notice and remember that when he says "Before, after, these two things", etc.,[26] he means there are five keywords: 'Before', 'After', 'Weak', 'Strong', and 'Within'. On these words is built the entire art of Master Liechtenauer, and they're the core and the fixed foundation of all fencing (on horse or on foot, armored or unarmored).

---

[25] Verse 9.
[26] Verse 17.

With the word 'Before', he means to always take and win the Leading Strike, † {whether it lands or not. (As Liechtenauer says, "Cut here and step there; charge toward him, hit or move on".[27])} When you approach by stepping or running, just as soon as you see you can reach your opponent with a step or a leap, then drive joyously toward wherever you see an exposure (toward his head or body, wherever you feel sure you can take him), boldly and fearlessly. In this way, you always win the Leading Strike, whether it goes well or poorly for him. Also, be certain and measured in your steps, so that you don't step too short nor too far.

Now, when you execute the Leading Strike (be it cutting or thrusting), if it succeeds, then quickly follow through. But if he defends against it, diverting your Leading Strike or otherwise defending with his sword, then as long as you remain on his sword, while you're being led away from the exposure you had targeted, you should feel precisely and notice whether he's Hard or Soft, and Strong or Weak on your sword (in his covering and diverting of your cut or thrust).

Thus, you fully feel how he is in his action. If he's Hard and Strong Within it, then as you fully feel and notice this, become Soft and Weak during and Within it, and before his cover is complete, execute a Following Strike. In other words, you immediately strike while he's still defending himself and covering your Leading Strike (be it cutting or thrusting). Then seek out other plays and rules, and with those, again step and strike toward his exposures.

Thus, you're continually in motion and in contact, so that you confuse and cheat your opponent amid his covering and defense, and he has too much work covering himself and

---

[27] Verse 6.

cannot win the Leading or Following Strikes. When he must cover himself and fixate on your strikes, he's always in greater danger than you: he must continue to defend himself or allow himself to be struck, and thus can only make his own strikes with great pain.

This is why Liechtenauer says "I say to you honestly, no man covers himself without danger. If you have understood this, he cannot come to blows".[28] You must thus fence according to the five words, which this statement and the whole of fencing are based on.

(Thus, a peasant may end up slaying a master simply because he's bold and wins the Leading Strike, as this teaching describes.)

[29]By the word 'Before', as we read earlier, he means to step in or charge, boldly and fearlessly, with a good Leading Strike (or with any initial strike) aiming toward the exposures of his head or body.

Whether you land it or not, you will still succeed at dazzling and frightening him so that he doesn't know what to do against this, and cannot recover or come to his senses before you immediately do a Following Strike, and thus you continually force him to defend and cover, so that he cannot come to his own blows.

If you do the first strike or Leading Strike and he succeeds in defending, then in his defense and covering, he could always deliver a Following Strike faster than you (even though you had the first one). He could immediately cut, or drive in

---

[28] Verses 40-41 and 100-101.
[29] The text beginning with this paragraph and going to the next piece of Recital are written on pages inserted late in the creation process.

with his pommel, or send **crosswise cuts** (which are always reliable), or he could just throw his sword forward crosswise (and with that, enter other plays), or begin something else before you get the chance to continue.

(It's written further on how one play grows from another such that your opponent cannot get away unbeaten, as long as you follow this teaching.)

† {So, perform the Leading Strike and the Following Strike as one idea and as though they were a single attack, one promptly and swiftly following the other.}

When it happens that someone defends against the Leading Strike, he must defend with his sword, and in this way, he must always come onto your sword. If he's late and unready in his defense, then remain on his sword and immediately wind, and feel precisely and notice whether he wants to pull back from your sword.

Once you're engaged with each other on the sword and have extended your points toward each other's exposures, if he pulls himself back, then before he can recover from your strike, immediately follow through with a good thrust toward his chest with your point (or otherwise forward toward wherever you can land the surest and closest hit) in such a way that he cannot escape from your sword without harm, because when you immediately follow like this you get closer and closer to him, and with that, you direct your point forward on his sword toward whatever's nearest and closest.

Thus, even if your opponent cuts or thrusts wildly around as he pulls back, you can always come faster into the Following Strike (cutting or thrusting) before he comes to his first one.

Now, with the word 'After', Liechtenauer means that when you have made the Leading Strike, you should deliver a

Following Strike in the same movement (immediately and without pause), and be always in motion and in contact, and always do one after another. If your first strike fails, then the second, the third, or the fourth lands, and your opponent is never allowed to come to blows. No one can have greater advantage in fencing than he who executes the five words according to this lesson.

But if, once you have come onto his sword, your opponent remains on your sword with his defense and covering, and you also remain on his sword and haven't yet delivered a Following Strike, then stay on his sword and wind, and feel precisely and notice whether he's Strong or Weak on your sword.

If you feel and notice that he's Hard, Strong, and firm, and wants to press on your sword, then be Soft and Weak against him and give way to his strength, and allow your sword to be swept out and driven away by his pushing. Then quickly and rapidly divert and pull your sword back, and drive swiftly against his exposures, toward his head or body, with cutting, thrusting, and slicing (however you find the nearest and surest way).

Because the harder and surer he pushes in and forces with his sword while you're Soft and Weak against it, giving way to him and allowing your sword to go aside, the more and the further his sword also goes aside, and he becomes quite exposed. Then you can strike and injure him as you want before he recovers himself before your cut or thrust.

However, if you feel and notice that he's Soft and Weak on your sword, then be Hard and Strong against him, and charge forward with your point firmly on his sword and drive toward his exposures (whichever is closest), just as though a cord or a thread were tied to the point of your sword which would lead it to his nearest exposure.

With this thrust, you become well aware of whether he's Weak, letting his sword be pushed aside and letting himself be hit, or he's Strong, defending and diverting your thrust.

If he's Strong on the sword, defending against your thrust and diverting the sword, then become Soft and Weak against it once again, giving way to him and letting your sword be pushed aside, and then swiftly seek his exposures with cutting, thrusting, and slicing (whichever it may be). This is what Liechtenauer means by the words 'Hard' and 'Soft'.

This is based on the classical authorities: as Aristotle wrote in his book *Peri Hermeneias*: "Opposites positioned near each other shine greater, and opposites which are adjoined are augmented".[30] Thus, Strong against Weak, Hard against Soft, and vice versa. The stronger always wins when strength goes against strength, but Liechtenauer fences according to the true and correct art, so a weak man wins more surely with his art and cunning than a strong man with his strength. Otherwise, what's the point of art?

Therefore, fencer, learn to feel well; as Liechtenauer says "Learn the feeling; 'Within', that word cuts sore-ly".[31] When you're on his sword, and you feel well whether he's Strong or Weak on your sword, then during and Within this, you can well consider and know what to do against him (according to the aforementioned art and teaching). For truly, he can't pull back from the sword without harm: as Liechtenauer

---

[30] This doesn't match any recognizable Aristotelian quotation, though the idea is present in many places in his work.
[31] Verse 78.

says, "Strike in so that it snaps at whoever pulls back in front of you".[32]

If you act firmly according to this lesson, you will always take and win the Leading Strike, and as soon as you execute it, charge in with a Following Strike immediately and without delay (that is, the second, third, or fourth strike, whether it be a cut or a thrust), so that he can never come to blows. If you should come onto the sword with him, be certain in your feeling and do as was written earlier.

The foundation of fencing is to always be in motion and to not delay, and fencing is also based on feeling, so *if you are able*, do as stated before and always have measure and moderation in all that you begin and do. If you win the Leading Strike, don't deliver it so impetuously or aggressively that you can't deliver a Following Strike afterward.

This is why Liechtenauer says "Thus you will see, all things have measure and moderation".[33] You should also understand this when stepping, and in all other plays and rules of fencing, etc.

---

[32] Verse 99.
[33] Verse 12.

This is the text in which he names the five strikes and the other pieces of his fencing.

21   Learn five strikes,
      To the guard from the right.[34]

23   Wrath cut curves thwarts,
      Has glancing with parts.

24   While the fool will parry,
      Pursue, overrun, stab and harry.

25   Pull back and disengage,
      Run through, press hands, and slice away.

26   Hang and wind to exposures below and above,
      Strike and catch, sweep, and thrust with a shove.

---

[34] Verse 22 is omitted for unknown reasons. It states, "And this we can promise, / Your art will be glorious."

This is about the wrathful cut, etc.

27   Who cuts from above in any way,
      The wrathful cut's point keeps him at bay.

28   If he sees and fends you off,
      Be fearless, take it off above.

29   Wind and thrust if he holds strong so;
      If he sets you off, take it below.

30   Now remember this part:
      Cut and thrust, lay Soft or Hard;

31   Within the Before and the After,
      Be careful, and do not rush to the war.

32   Those who rashly seek the bind,
      Shame above and below is all they'll find.

33   Howsoever you will wind,
      Cut, thrust, slice you seek to find.

34   Further, you should learn to choose
      Which of them should best suit you.

35   In whatever way you've bound,
      Many masters you'll confound.

xi   Do not cut toward his sword,
      But rather seek his exposures.

xvi   Toward his head, toward his body,
      If you wish to remain unharmed.

xvii Whether you hit or you miss,
      Always target his exposures.

xviii * {In every lesson,
      Turn your point against his exposures.

xix   Whoever swings around widely,
      He will often be shamed severely.

xx   Toward the nearest exposure,
      Cut and thrust with suddenness.

xxi   And also step always
        Toward your right side with it,
xxii   So you may begin
        Fencing or wrestling with advantage.}

Gloss. Here notice and remember that when you cut over him straight from your shoulder, Liechtenauer calls this the **wrathful cut**, because when you're in your fury and wroth, there's no other cut as ready as this blow (straight from your shoulder toward the man).

By this, Liechtenauer means that when someone begins to cut over you, counter it by **cutting wrathfully** in and then firmly shoot your point against him. If he defends against your thrust, then swiftly take it away above and drive suddenly to the other side of his sword. But if he defends again, then be Hard and Strong against him on his sword, and swiftly and boldly wind and thrust. If he defends against this thrust, then take off again and quickly throw a cut below toward his legs (or wherever you can).

In this way, you continuously do one strike after another so that he cannot come to his own plays. Always keep the earlier keywords in mind ('Before' and 'After', 'Within', 'Strong' and 'Weak'), as well as cutting, stabbing, and slicing, and by no means forget them in your fight.

Also, don't rush with the **war**, because if an attack that you aim above fails then you should hit below.

(It's written further on how one strike makes itself out of another according to the legitimate art, regardless of whether it be cutting, thrusting, or slicing.)

Don't cut toward his sword, but rather toward him (toward his head or toward his body, wherever you can, etc.), and consider that the first verse could state "Whomever you cut over **wrathfully**, the point of the **wrathful cut** threatens him", etc.[35]

Simply act according to this teaching and always be in motion; either you hit or you miss, but he cannot come to blows (and with your striking, always step out well to the side).

Also remember that there are only two cuts (that is, over and under both sides), and all other cuts come from them regardless of how they're named.

These are the pinnacle and the foundation of all other cuts, and they, in turn, come from and depend on the point of the sword, which is the center and the core of all other plays (as was written well earlier).

{From these same cuts come the **four parries** from both sides, with which you disrupt and counter all cutting and thrusting, and all guards. From them, you also come into the **four hangers**, from which you can perform the art well (as is written further on).}

However you fence, your point should ever and always be turned against your opponent's face or chest, so that he's constantly frustrated and concerned that you'll arrive faster than him because your path to him is shorter. If it happens that you win the Leading Strike, then be secure, certain, and quick with this turning, and as soon as you have thus turned, immediately begin to drive agilely and courageously.

Your point should always seek your opponent's chest, turning and positioning itself against it (as is written better further on). As soon as you come upon someone's sword, your

---

[35] Verse 27.

point should never be more than three hand-breadths[36] away from his face or chest, and take care that it will arrive on the most direct path and not travel widely around, so that your opponent cannot arrive first.

Don't allow yourself to become relaxed or hesitant, nor defend too lazily, nor be willing to go too widely or too far around.

Followed by one blank page.

---

[36] Literally "half an ell"; the length of a Medieval ell varies by town and region, but is generally based on either the length someone's elbow to fingertips, or six times the width of someone's hand. I find the hand-breadth measure to be easier to visualize.

This is about the four exposures, etc., etc.

36   Four exposures know,
           To truly guide your blow.

37   Without fear or doubt,
           For what he'll bring about.

Gloss. Here remember that Liechtenauer divides a man into four parts, as if he drew a line on his body from his part downward to between his legs, and another line on his body along his belt.[37] In this way, four quarters arise: one right and one left above the belt, and the same below the belt. These are the **four exposures**, which each have their particular techniques.

Never target the sword, only the exposures.

---

[37] Note that Medieval people generally wore their belts at the top of their waists, meaning at their navels or just below their ribs.

How to break the four exposures.

38 Redeem yourself by taking
     Four exposures by their breakings.

39 To above, you redouble,
     Transmute low without trouble.

40 Now do not forget,
     No one defends without a threat.

41 If this is well known,
     Rarely will he come to blows.

This is about the crooked cut, etc.

42   Throw the curve, and don't be slow,
      Onto his hands your point should go.

43   Many strikes you will offset,
      With a curve and with good steps.

44   Cut the curve to the flat,
      Weaken masters with that.

45   When it clashes above,
      Step off, that I will love.

46   Cut short, and curve not,
      If the changing through is sought.

47   Curve who'd distress you,
      Confuse, bind, and press him,

48   Give him no way to know
      Where he's safe from your blow.

Gloss. Here notice and remember that the **crooked cut** comes down from above and goes in a **curved** way with a good step outward to one side.

This is why Liechtenauer says that if you want to bring this cut well, step well to your right, fully flanking him with your cut, and cut in a **curved** manner, swiftly and well, and then throw or shoot your point over his hilt and over his hands.

Cut ~~toward his~~ with your flat; if you hit ~~the flat,~~ his sword[38] then remain Strongly on it and press firmly, and see what you can

---

[38] "With your" and "his sword" are inserted over the deletions and seem intended to replace them. However, the deletions describe the typical teaching of the curved cut, whereas the insertions seem to represent a unique idea or teaching. For this reason, unlike other instances of deletion, both the original and the replacement text are translated here for comparison.

bring in the quickest and most decisive way, with cutting, thrusting, or slicing.

By no means should you cut too shortly, but if you do, then don't forget the **changing through**.

Followed by one blank page.

There's a cut called the **avoidance** (as it's written after the **crosswise cut**), which comes from the **curved cut** and should come before the **crosswise cut**, and it attacks **crookedly** and obliquely from below and shoots the point in over his hilt, just as the **curved cut** does down from above.

#

53   Avoid and mislead,
       And hit low where you please.

54   The inverter equips you,
       To run through and grip, too.

55   Take the elbow to bring
       Him off balance, and spring.

56   Avoid twice;
       If you touch, make a slice.

57   Double it and on it goes,
       Step in left and don't be slow.

xxiii   Because all fencing
       Will by rights have speed,

xiii   And also audacity,
       Prudence, cunning, and ingenuity.

This is about the crosswise cut, etc.

49   What comes from the sky,
           The cross takes in its stride.

50   Cut across with the strong,
           And be sure to work on.

51   To the plow drive across,
           Yoke it hard to the ox.

52   Take a leap and cross well,
           And his head is imperiled.

Gloss. Here notice and remember that out of the whole art of the sword, no cut is as good, as honest, as ready, and as fierce as the **crosswise cut**. It goes **across** to both sides, with both edges (the front and the back), to all exposures (upper and lower), and when you **cut across** correctly, you counter and defend against everything that comes from above (meaning the high cuts and whatever else goes downward from above).

When you bring or throw the sword forward well, it **crosses** in front of your head to whichever side you want, just as if you were to come into the upper hangers or winds, except that when you **cut across**, the flats of the sword are what turns: the one above or upward, and the other downward or below, and the edges go to the sides, one **crossing** to the right side and the other to the left side.

It's very good to come onto your opponent's sword with this **crosswise cut**, and when you get onto his sword, no matter how it happens, he can only escape from you with great difficulty.

You can also strike toward both sides with **crosswise cuts**, and as you bring the **crosswise cut** to either side, above or below, your sword should go up with the hilt above you and with your hands thrown forward in front of your head, so that you're well covered and defended.

Now, you should bring the **crosswise cut** with a certain strength, and when you must fight for your neck, use the teaching written previously so that you win the Leading Strike with a good **crosswise cut**.

When you approach him, as soon as you see that you can reach him with a step or a leap, then cut across with your back edge, from above toward his head from your right side, and let your point shoot and then **cross** well so that your point goes well and winds or turns around his head like a belt. Thus, if you **cross** well with a good leap or step to the side, he can only turn it away or cover himself with difficulty.

Once you win the Leading Strike with a **crosswise cut** to one side, no matter whether you hit or miss, immediately win the Following Strike in a single advance, at once and with no delay, with a **crosswise cut** to the other side (with the forward edge), before he manages to recover and come to blows (according to the teaching written previously).

Also, **cross** to both sides, toward the **ox** and toward the **plow** (that is, toward the upper and lower exposures), from one side to the other, above and below, continuously and without delay, so that you're always in motion and don't let him come to blows.

As often as you **cut across**, above or below, you should strike well and throw the sword **crosswise** high in front of your head so that you're well covered.

Followed by one blank page.

This is about the glancing cut.

58	The glancer disrupts
	What the buffalo cuts or thrusts.
59	The glancer endangers
	Whoever threatens the changer.
60	If he looks short to you,
	Defeat him by changing through.
61	To the point your glance goes,
	Take his neck boldly so.
62	Glance up high instead
	To endanger his hands and head.
xxiv	**#** {Glance to the right,
	If you want to fence well.
xxv	The glancing cut I prize,
	If it doesn't come too lazily.}

Gloss. Here notice and remember that the **glancing cut** comes down from your right side with the back edge. It goes to the left side, **aslant** or askew, while stepping out to the right side with turned sword and overturned hand.

This same cut counters everything that a **buffalo** (that is, a peasant) will cut down from above, as they often do, and also counters the same as the **crosswise cut** (as was described previously).

Whoever threatens to **change through** will be put to shame by the **glancing cut**. But see that you **glance** well and long enough, and shoot the point firmly, otherwise you will be hindered by his **changing through**.

And **glance** with your point toward his throat without fear. And...[39]

---

[39] Text ends here abruptly.

When you see that, from scabbards,
Swords are being drawn,
Steady yourself therein,
And truly remember your steps.
Before and After: these two things
Explore, and also learn to leap away.
Pursue in all encounters
If you wish to dupe the strong.
If he defends, then pull back and thrust.
If he defends, move into him.
The winding and the hanging,
Learn to artfully bring forth.
And probe his intentions
Test if he is Hard or Soft.
If he fights with strength
Then be artfully prepared,
And if he attacks wide or long,
Shooting in defeats him.
If, with Hard strikes,
He covers himself, strike without fear.
Cut here and step there;
Charge in, then hit or move on.
Do not cut toward his sword,
But rather seek his exposures.
Whether you hit or you miss,
Always target his exposures.
With both hands
Learn to bring your point to his eyes
Fence with good sense,
And always win the Leading Strike;
Whether you hit or miss,
Strike immediately at his exposure with the Following Strike.

The Gloss

And also step always
Toward the right-hand side with it,
So you may begin
Fencing or wrestling with advantage.[40]

---

[40] At first glance, this appears to be a poem of the author's own devising, but many of the verses are based on couplets from Liechtenauer's Recital (the ones written in red ink); the couplets in red italics are based on those of the Recital on armored fencing. The lines in black text are original, but several of them appear elsewhere in this gloss and only three couplets are completely unique.

This is a fine example of the Medieval practice of using the text of a mnemonic (like the Recital) to teach different, distinct lessons, through paraphrase and reorganization. Here, he seems to have stitched together fragments from those sources in order to present a new teaching: a general lesson on fencing from the draw.

Because the verses are rarely in their exact normal form, the rhyming translation has not been used and instead they are translated more literally.

This is about the part cut, etc.

63   Strike from your part
      And threaten his face with art.

64   When it turns it will set
      On his chest with great threat.

65   What the parter brings forth,
      The crown drives it off,

66   So slice through the crown,
      And you break it well down.

67   Press the sweeping attacks,
      With a slice and pull back.

xxv   The part cut I prize,
      If it doesn't come too lazily.

Followed by three blank pages.

*Liechtenauer holds **four lairs** only, because they proceed from the upper and lower hangers and you can surely bring techniques from them.*[41]

This is about the four lairs, etc.

68   Lie in four lairs,
             And the others forswear.

69   Ox and plow, and the fool too,
             And the day should not be unknown to you.

Gloss. Here he names the **four lairs** or four guards. There is little is to say about them; primarily, that you shouldn't lie in them for too long. This is why Liechtenauer has a particular proverb, "Whoever lies still, he is dead; whoever moves, he yet lives".[42] This applies to the **lairs**, that you should rouse yourself with techniques rather than wait in the guards and in this way miss your chance.

The first guard, the **plow**, is when you lay your point on the ground, in front of you or at your side. After **setting off**, this is also called the **barrier guard** or the **iron gate**.

The second guard, the **ox**, is the upper hanger from the shoulder.

xxvi   The fool always counters
             What the man cuts or thrusts

xxvii   With hangers, sweeps,
             Pursuit, and simultaneous parries.

---

[41] There is no insertion point indicated for this text, so it is presumably not an accidental omission, but a later addition or comment.

[42] This proverb doesn't come from the Recital and doesn't appear in any other source in the Liechtenauer tradition.

The third guard, the **fool**, is the lower hanger. With it, you can counter all cuts and thrusts well.

The fourth guard, from **the day**, is also the **long point**. Whoever leads it well with extended arms cannot be hit easily with cutting nor thrusting. It can also be called "the hanger above the head".

Also understand that you counter all the **lairs** and guards with cutting, so that as you cut boldly toward someone, he must flinch and cover himself. This is why Liechtenauer doesn't say much about the **lairs** or guards, but rather maintains that you should be concerned with winning the Leading Strike before your opponent can (*as you are able*).

This is about the four parries, etc., etc.

70   The parries are four,
        They leave lairs well sored.

71   Of parrying, beware:
        You should not be caught there.

72   If parrying befalls you,
        As it can happen to do,

73   Hear now what I say:
        Wrench off, slice away!

74   Set upon to four extents;
        Stay thereon if you want to end.

xxviii   **#** {*Many strikes you'll hurt and harry*
        If you fence with proper parries,[43]

xxix   Because when you parry,
        You come swiftly into the hangers.}

Gloss. Here remember that there are **four parries** to both sides, one upper and one lower to each side, and they counter or disrupt all **lairs** and guards. Any way that you divert or deflect someone's cut, thrust, or slice with your sword, from above or from below, could well be called **parrying**.

If you're the one **parried**, however that happens, swiftly pull back and cut again in a single advance.

If you **parry** or turn away someone's cut or thrust, immediately step in and follow through on his sword so that he cannot pull back. Then do whatever you can, but if you hesitate and delay, it will be harmful to you.

Also wind well and always turn your point against his chest so that he must constantly worry about it.

---

[43] This verse is phrased similarly to 43.

Learn to come onto the sword of your opponent, which you can do well with these **parries**, because they come from the four cuts (one over and one under each side) and become the **four hangers**. As soon as you parry above or below, you should immediately arrive in the hangers.

Just as you turn away all cuts and thrusts with the front edge, it's the same with **parrying**.

This is about pursuit, etc., etc.

75	Learn the twofold pursuit,
	And the guard, to slice through.
76	The ways to lead out are double,
	From there work and struggle.
77	And determine what he seeks,
	Hard or Soft in his techniques.
78	Learn to feel with discipline;
	The word that cuts deepest is 'Within'.
79	Learn the pursuit twice,
	If it touches, make a good old slice.
xxx	In whatever way you've bound,
	All the strong you will confound.[44]
xviii	In every lesson,
	Turn your point against his face.
xxxi	Pursue with your entire body
	So that your point stays on.
xxxii	Also learn to swiftly wrench,
	So you may end well.

---

[44] This verse is phrased similarly to both 35 and 90.

This is about crossing over. Fencer, notice it.

80 Whoever aims to take it below,
    By the crossing over, their folly show.

81 When it clashes above,
    Remain Strong, that I will love.

82 See your work be done,
    Or press doubly hard upon.

xxxiii Whoever presses you down,
        Cross over him and strike sharply again.

xxxiv From both sides cross over,
       And remember the slices.

This is about setting off. Learn this well.

83   The setting off, learn to do,
      That cuts and thrusts be ruined before you.

84   Whoever makes a thrust at you,
      Your point meets his and breaks it through.

85   From the right and from the left,
      Always meet him if you'll step.

xviii   In every lesson,
        Turn your point against his face.

This is about changing through, etc., etc.

86   Learn to change through,
             And cruelly thrust on both sides too.

87   All of those who seek the bind,
             Changing through will surely find.

xxxv   † {When you have changed through,
             strike, thrust, or wind, be not lax.

xxxvi   Do not cut toward his sword,
             change through and seek with that.}

Gloss. Here remember that the **changing through** goes directly to both sides (down from above and up from below) if you otherwise do it quickly.

If you want to **change through** from your right side (down from above), then hew from above directly toward him so that you shoot your point toward his left side, above his hilt, and aim for the little gap or window between his edge and his hilt. If you hit, you have won.

If he defends against this by turning aside your point and pressing it away with his sword, then let your point sink down under his sword, from that side around to the other. This shouldn't go widely around, but as closely as possible below his sword so that you can then drive in swiftly over his hilt with a good thrust. When you feel it land, follow through well. As you do on one side, from above and from below, do the same from the other side.

Also, when someone binds with you, charge forward on his sword with your point toward his exposure. If he defends, **change through** as before, or wind and feel whether his intention is Hard or Soft. Thereafter, seek his exposures with cutting, thrusting, or slicing.

The Gloss

This is about pulling back. Fencer, remember.

88   Step up close into the bind,
              Pull back, and what you seek you'll find.

89   Pull back, and if he meets, pull more,
              Work and find what makes him sore.

90   Pull back whenever you are bound,
              And many masters you'll confound.

xxxvii   Pull back from the sword
              And carefully consider your way.

This is about running through, notice now.

91	Run through, hang it to the floor
	By the pommel, then bring grips for sure.
92	For those who strongly approach you,
	Do remember the running through.
xxxviii	Run through and shove.
	Invert if he grabs for the hilt.

This is about slicing off, etc., etc.

93   When it's firm, slice away,
            From below, you slice both ways.

94   And the slices, they number four,
            Two below; above, two more.

xxxix   Slice whoever will cross you,
            To eagerly avoid injury.

xl   Do not slice in fright,
            First consider wrenching.

xli   You can slice well in any crossing,
            If you omit the wrenching.

xlii   If you wish to remain unharmed,
            Then don't move with the slicing.

This is about pressing the hands, etc., etc.

95   Turn your edge just like that,
           Press his hands onto the flat.

xliii   One thing is turning,
           Another is twisting, the third is hanging.

xliv   If you want to make fencers despair,
           Then always press while shoving.

xlv   Over his hands,
           Cut and slice swiftly.

xlvi   Also draw the slices
           Above, over his head.

xlvii   Whoever presses the hands
           Pulls his fingers back without injury.

Know that as soon as you turn away his cut or thrust with your edge, you should immediately step in and drive quickly toward him. If you wait and delay, you will suffer injury.

Also notice and remember that you turn away all cuts and thrusts with the forward edge of your sword, from the middle of the edge to the hilt. As soon as you have turned your forward edge into it, then the closer a cut or thrust comes to your hilt, the better and more powerfully you can turn away these cuts or thrusts: the closer to the hilt, the stronger and mightier, and the closer to the point, the weaker and feebler.

Therefore, if you want to be a good fencer, learn above all other things to turn away well, so that as you do so, you come immediately to the winds, from which you can perform the entire art and beauty of fencing.

The forward edge of the sword is called the true edge, and all cuts and thrusts are spoiled by its turning.

This is about hanging. Fencer, learn this, etc.

96	There are the two ways to hang:
	From the ground, from your hand.
97	In every attack, whether cut or a thrust,
	The Hard and the Soft lies within, you can trust.
98	In the window freely stand,
	Watch his manner close at hand.
99	Whoever pulls back,
	Strike in with a snap.
100	Now do not forget
	No one defends without a threat.
101	And if this is well-known,
	Rarely will he come to blows.
xlviii	As you remain,
	On the sword, then also make
xlix	Cuts, thrusts, or slices.
	Remember to feel into it
l	Without any preference.
	Also do not flee from the sword
li	Because masterful fencing
	Is rightly at the sword.
lii	Whoever binds on you,
	The war wrestles with him severely.
liii	The noble winding
	Can also surely find him.
liv	With cutting, with thrusting,
	And with slicing you surely find him.
[32]	*Howsoever you will wind,*
	Cut, thrust, slice you seek to find.
lv	And the noble hanging
	Should not be without the winding.

lvi   Because from the hangers
            You bring forth the winding.

Gloss. Here notice and remember that there are **two hangers** from each side, one over and one underneath. With them, you can come onto your opponent's sword well, ✝ {because they come from high and low cuts}.

If it happens that you bind with someone, or otherwise come onto his sword, then remain on his sword and wind, and stay with him on the sword like that, boldly and in good spirit, without any fear.

Quite precisely wait, watch for, and notice well whatever he wants to do, or whatever he has in mind which he will perform against you. Liechtenauer calls remaining on the sword like this a **speaking window**. As you stay with him on the sword, feel well and notice his intention, whether it be Hard or Soft, and orient yourself accordingly (as it has often been written previously).

If he happens to pull back from your sword before you actually begin, then immediately follow through and send cuts or thrusts at him (whichever you can perform in the surest way, before he comes to anything else); ✝ {since you're closer to him as you remain on his sword, merely extend your point against him. Then when he pulls back, immediately follow him in with your point before he can perform a strike.} But if he remains with you on the sword, then test well and notice whether he's Hard or Soft on your sword.

If he's Soft and Weak, then swiftly and boldly go forth and attack with your Strength, pressing and pushing away his sword. Then seek his exposures, toward his head or body (whatever you can get).

But if he's Hard and Strong on your sword and wants to press and push you aside firmly, then be Soft and Weak against his Strength, and weaken his Strength and his pressure with your sword.

As you weaken and his sword goes aside (as was also written earlier), then before he can recover, seek his exposures with cutting, thrusting, or slicing (however you can get to him in the surest manner), swiftly, rapidly, and boldly (in accordance with the teaching written earlier), so that he cannot cut nor thrust, nor otherwise come to blows.

This is why Liechtenauer says "I say to you honestly, no man covers himself without danger. If you have understood this, he cannot come to blows."[45] By this, he means that no one can protect himself from you without fear or injury, if you act according to the teaching written earlier: if you take and win the Leading Strike, then he must either continually defend himself or let himself be struck.

If you deliver the Leading Strike, whether you land it or not, then quickly deliver a Following Strike in a single advance, before he can come to blows. Indeed, if you want to deliver the Leading Strike, you must also deliver a Following Strike as if in one thought and intention, as though you would deliver them simultaneously if that weren't impossible.

This is what Liechtenauer means by "Before and after, these two things", etc.[46] If you deliver the Leading Strike, whether you land it or not, then also do a Following Strike at once, swiftly and rapidly, so that he cannot come to blows. In this way, you can preempt him at all matters of fencing.

---

[45] Verses 100-101 (also 40-41).
[46] Verse 17.

Now, as soon as you get to him first and win the Leading Strike, immediately deliver a Following Strike. Don't deliver the Leading Strike if you don't have an intended Following Strike in mind; be always in motion and never idling nor delaying. Always do one after another, swiftly and rapidly, so that he comes to nothing. If you do this correctly, then anyone who gets away from you without being hit must be very good indeed.

With this art or this advantage, it often happens that a peasant or untrained man beats a good master, because he delivers the Leading Strike and charges in boldly; it may be lightly overlooked, but it hits Within and thus strikes him and puts him to shame. This is because it's more dangerous to wait to defend and receive strikes than to attack and win the Leading Strike. Therefore, arrange to be first in all matters of fencing, and to come well to the right side of your opponent, and then you can be more sure of everything than he.

Followed by one blank page.

[This is about winding]⁴⁷

108   On both sides this applies:
Learn to step with eight winds.

106   And each wind of the blade
Into three can be made:

107   Twenty-four can be named,
Though they're one and the same.

105   And eight winds there are,
If you rightly regard,

lviii   And learn to lead them well,
So you may hit the four exposures.

lix   Because each exposure
Can be hit in six ways.

---

⁴⁷ This is the only place in the treatise where verses from the Recital are presented out of order. Furthermore, verses 102-104 are omitted entirely, as is 109 (though 109 is itself a repetition of verse 77). Here is the original sequence:

If you lead well, and counter right,
And finally, it's in your sight,
You must divide things as they are,
Into three wounders, each apart.
Hang the point in true and fair,
Wind your sword then well from there.
And eight winds there are,
If you rightly regard,
And each wind of blade
Into three can be made:
Twenty-four can be named,
Though they're one and the same.
On both sides this applies:
Learn to step with eight winds.
And determine what he seeks,
Hard or Soft in his techniques.

Gloss. Notice here that the winds are the correct art and the foundation of all the fencing with the sword, from which all other techniques and plays come.

It's difficult to be a good fencer without the winds, though certain dancing masters dismiss them and say that what comes from the winds is quite weak, and call it "from the shortened sword", because they are simple and go naively. They mean that techniques from the long sword should be done with extended arms and extended sword, and that they come aggressively and strongly with full strength of body but lacking good stance, and it's terrible to watch when someone stretches himself out as if he were trying to chase a rabbit.

If there were no art then the strong would always win, but this is not the way, neither in winding nor in the art of Liechtenauer, because this art doesn't require great strength.

The Gloss

Note: Here we jump forward fourteen folia to 64r. It's un-clear if the author thought of this as part of his gloss or not, but it is an attempt at a summary of the teachings of Liechtenauer, so it seems worthy of inclusion in this book. In between are a treatise by four other masters with some association to Liechtenauer (43ʳ-52ᵛ), and an un-glossed ren-dition of Liechtenauer's Recital on mounted (53ʳ-59ᵛ) and ar-mored fencing (60ʳ-62ʳ).

Here we explore and elaborate the pieces and rules of the un-armored fencing of Master Liechtenauer, using shorter and simpler speech for more and better learning and comprehen-sion. If the rhymes and glosses written earlier were unclear or hard to understand, here it will be recapped with short and simple advice.

First of all, notice and remember that Liechtenauer's fenc-ing relies on five words: 'Before', 'After', 'Strong', 'Weak', and 'Within'. These are the basis, core, and foundation of all fencing. No matter how much you fence, if you lack this foundation, you will often be put to shame despite your art. These words were often explained earlier, as they only sig-nify this: to always be in motion and to not rest or idle, so that your opponent cannot come to blows.

'Before' and 'After' signify the Leading Strike and the Fol-lowing Strike (as it was often written earlier), and this con-cerns what's called *principium et finis* (beginning and end). If you're a good, serious fencer, you fence with someone be-cause you want to defeat him with your art and not be de-feated yourself, and you cannot do this without the beginning and the end. Thus, if you want to begin well then you should be the one who takes and wins the Leading Strike well, not the one who doesn't, since if you strike at someone, you're more secure and better protected from cuts than he is (since he must watch out for and receive your strike).

When you take and win the Leading Strike, no matter if it lands or misses, then immediately and without pause, in a single advance, deliver a Following Strike (that is, a second strike, a third, a fourth, or a fifth), cutting or thrusting, so that you're always in motion and do one after another without pause, so that you never let him come to blows.

This is what Liechtenauer means by "I say to you honestly, no man covers himself without danger." (*without damage*) "If you have understood this, he cannot come to blows."[48] Do what was often written earlier and stay in motion.

The word 'Within' is related to the words 'Before' and 'After', since when one of you delivers the Leading Strike and the other defends against it, then during and Within the covering and defense, you can come to the Following Strike well.

The word 'Within' is also related to the words 'Strong' and 'Weak' (meaning feeling), since when you're on the sword with someone and you feel whether he's Strong or Weak, only then can you do according to the oft-written teaching.

Above all things, the foundation should have the principles of audacity, speed, prudence, intelligence, wisdom, etc., and also moderation in all things. If you win the Leading Strike, you shouldn't do it so recklessly that he can deliver a good Following Strike. Don't step too widely either, so that you can recover yourself well and take another step backward or forward if necessary.

---

[48] Verses 40-41 and 100-101

As Liechtenauer says, "Thus you will see, all things have measure and moderation".[49] Do not be hasty, consider well in advance what you want to do, and then do it boldly and swiftly toward your opponent's head or body, and never toward his sword.

When you cut with certainty toward his head or body (that is, toward the four exposures), then he often comes onto your sword without wanting to: when he covers himself, he covers himself with his sword, and thus he comes onto your sword.

This is what Liechtenauer means when he says:

xi	Do not cut toward his sword,
	But rather seek his exposures.
xvi	Toward his head, toward his body,
	If you wish to remain unharmed.
xvii	Whether you hit or you miss,
	Always target his exposures.
xviii	In every lesson,
	Turn your point against his exposures.
xix	Whoever swings around widely,
	He will often be shamed severely.
xx	Toward the nearest exposure,
	Cut and thrust with suddenness.
lx	And don't hold back,
	So he can't come before you do.
lxi	Thus you can stand your ground
	Against a good man.

---

[49] Verse 8.

Select Bibliography

Primary source

Germanisches Nationalmuseum, ms. 3227a.

Literature

A lot of important literature on the ms. 3227a has been published in German, but I am limiting this bibliography to English-language sources. For relevant German materials, you can consult their bibliographies.

ACUTT, JAMES (2010). *Knightly Martial Arts*. Lulu.com.

ALDERSON, KEITH (2014). "Arts and Crafts of War: *die Kunst des Schwerts* in its Manuscript Context." *"Can The Bones Come to Life?": Insights from Reconstruction, Reenactment, and Recreation*, Vol. 1. Wheaton, IL: Freelance Academy Press. pp 24-29.

BURKART, ERIC (2016). "The Autograph of an Erudite Martial Artist. A Close Reading of Nuremberg, Germanisches Nationalmuseum, Hs. 3227a." *Late Medieval and Early Modern Fight Books. Transmission and Tradition of Martial Arts in Europe (14th-17th Centuries)* (*History of Warfare*, vol. 112). Ed. DANIEL JAQUET, KARIN VERELST, and TIMOTHY DAWSON. Leiden: Brill. pp 451-480.

VODIČKA, ONDŘEJ (2019). "Origin of the oldest German Fencing Manual Compilation (GNM Hs. 3227a)." *Waffen- und Kostümkunde* 61(1): 87-108.

ŻABIŃSKI, GRZEGORZ (2008). "Unarmored Longsword Combat by Master Liechtenauer via Priest Döbringer." *Masters of Medieval and Renaissance Martial Arts*. Ed. JEFFREY HULL. Boulder, CO: Paladin Press. pp 59-116.

Acknowledgements

I will first thank KENDRA BROWN, not only for proofreading some of the first drafts of this translation, but also for putting up with being ignored for hours at a time as I worked on it (and reminding me to come up for air sometimes).

I also thank the proofreaders of various drafts, including KRISTEN ARGYLE, MATTIAS BRÄNNSTRÖM, JACK BERGGREN-ELERS, JACK GASSMAN, and CARRIE PATRICK.

This work is only possible due to the prior contributions of many, many scholars over the course of the past five decades, which slowly expanded our understanding and built up the foundation of knowledge that we take for granted.

I've already acknowledged prior work on this manuscript, but I will do so again: DIERK HAGEDORN and ONDŘEJ VODIČKA both undertook to transcribe this text and make it more readily accessible for us all.

My understanding of this manuscript was shaped by the translations and analysis of JAY ACUTT, JENS P. KLEINAU, DAVID LINDHOLM (and friends), THOMAS STOEPPLER, GRZEGORZ ŻABIŃSKI, and especially CHRISTIAN TROSCLAIR, whose generosity with his translation talents has been an enormous influence on not just this book, but our whole community. Without his efforts, Wiktenauer itself would be a shadow of what it is.

I thank my various training partners over the years in ARMA Provo, True Edge Academy, Forte Swordplay, the Cambridge HEMA Society, and Athena School of Arms, and the great fencers who have been my teachers, including JAKE NORWOOD, STEW FEIL, ELI COMBS, MIKE EDELSON, CORY WINSLOW, and NATHAN WESTON. Our community is a remarkable venture, and we have built remarkable things together.

And finally, thank you to all the people who have used and helped improve the Wiktenauer. Were it not for my successes there, I don't know that I would still be doing HEMA today.

About the Author

Michael Chidester is the Editor-in-Chief of Wiktenauer and, as Director of the Wiktenauer, an officer of the non-profit HEMA Alliance.

Michael has been studying historical European martial arts since 2001. He was a member of the Association for Renaissance Martial Arts until 2006, where he achieved the rank of general Free Scholar, and he acted as the ARMA Provo Study Group Leader from 2007 until its dissolution in 2009. Michael co-founded the True Edge Academy of Swordsmanship in 2009, and until late 2010 was senior instructor at its Provo, Utah branch.

In 2012, Michael was appointed to the newly-established position of Director of the Wiktenauer by the HEMA Alliance general council, formalizing the role of principal designer and editor that he had assumed in early 2010. As Wiktenauer lead, Michael has assembled the most complete catalog of HEMA manuscripts currently available, including such resources as scans, transcriptions, and translations, and is currently laboring to assemble a similar catalog of printed treatises. In 2013, these efforts earned him a HEMA Scholar Award for Best Supporting Researcher.

Michael has lectured on Medieval and Renaissance martial arts at the *Historical Swordplay Symposium* at the Massachusetts Center for Interdisciplinary Renaissance Studies (including offering the keynote in 2014), *Life, the Universe, & Everything: the Marion K. "Doc" Smith Symposium* at Brigham Young University, and numerous HEMA events in Europe and America including *Blood on the River*, *Broken Point*, *Fechtschule America*, *Fechtschule New York*, *HEMAG Dijon*, the *Iron Gate Exhibition*, *Longpoint*, *Meyer Sympo-*

sium, the *Purpleheart Armory Open, Swordsquatch*, and the *Western Martial Arts Workshop*.

He has authored or edited various books, including *The Flower of Battle: MS M.383* (forthcoming), *"...eyn Grunt und Kern aller Künsten des Fechtens": The Long Sword Gloss of GNM Manuscript 3227a* (2020), *The Illustrated Meyer* (2019), *The Recital of the Chivalric Art of Fencing of the Grand Master Johannes Liechtenauer* (2015), and *The Flower of Battle of Master Fiore de'i Liberi, Volume I* and *Volume II* (2015).

In 2010, Michael received a Bachelor of Arts in Philosophy from Brigham Young University, with minor degrees in Logic and Military Science and additional coursework in Italian and Spanish. He developed a certain fluency in the latter while living abroad in Mexico from 2002 to 2004.

Michael is a Research Scholar of the Meyer Freifechter Guild, a founding member of the Society for Historical European Martial Arts Studies (SHEMAS), a member of the Western Martial Arts Coalition (WMAC), and a Lifetime Member of the HEMA Alliance.

CPSIA information can be obtained
at www.ICGtesting.com
Printed in the USA
BVHW041332170621
609824BV00012B/2283

9 781953 683137